32 YEARS APART

a mother and her child

BREINDA CROSBY-AVERHART
and
BRANDI KNEEDLY

DEDICATION

To Larry Crosby, Sr.

CONTENTS

ACKNOWLEDGEMENTS

We would like to thank all Mental Health Professionals for your continuous dedication to giving back to your communities in a meaningful way.

INTRODUCTION

May 09, 1987 was the first time I met Brandi Lavada Kneedly. Tight-fisted and fragile. I could not believe that I was the mother of this bundle of joy. Time progressed, and so did my love for her.

Brandi was a courageous child. She was always telling me, "Mommy make mistakes!" or "Mommy, I can do it!" My family and I began to call her Ms. Can Do.

Hailing from a musical family, I was certain that my daughter would be talented. Her talent showed up sooner than I expected. In first grade, my child was saying words while tapping her little feet. The words and the toe-tapping sounds were rhythmic and steady.

"Suga Mama, where you get those sounds from?"

"Mommy, I did it!" Ms. Can Do does it again.

The past two years have been horrific. All the killings of black people in America were taking up my good space. Then there was the murder of George Floyd, which was an American tragedy that should have never occurred. The way he was killed will stay with me forever and a day. It was an affront to humanity.

Subsequently, COVID-19 came to our shores, taking the lives of so many people. This pandemic invaded every country.

For a long time, I was unable to see Brandi. Therefore, we talked over the phone and texted daily. I am grateful for technology.

Brandi and I decided to write a book together in an attempt to make sense of these times. Until we were able to see one another, we wrote in journals, called one another, and critiqued our work.

We were the inspiration each of us needed to continue our quest.

After getting our vaccinations, we finally came together in person to collaborate on this project. We sat at the kitchen table by candlelight and wrote and shared. Many days passed until our book of poetry was finished.

YOU ARE SEEN

It's just us.

Our pain,

Our hurts,

Wounds covered in mud

Clay hardening now.

And not a moment later.

Here they come,

Painting faces over our clay.

So they don't have to look at our hurt, our wounds have eyes that don't hide.

Eyes wide open.

Even our strength comes with a price.

They barely can stand to look me in

My beautiful brown eyes,

Their un-comfort with our truths

With our stories,

Have them recreating our stories with their fairy tales.

Write over our stories with their markers,

Correcting our Tea's and drafting our I's.

They turn the volume down on our voices,

So they can harmonize over our hymns.

Black child, I sit here holding your hand. Looking you in your eyes, you are seen here,

You beautifully made brown skin child.

Let me tell you. Your hurt is real

Your joy absolutely matters.

Overall your healing is precedent. Your truth is truth.

BLACK SWEAT

Deep beats vibrating through my bones.

Thick hips writing lyrics to a poem,

not even written yet.

To a beat, ears can't even hear

Only body can feel.

Beads of sweat traveling from the brow of my forehead to the side of my
rotating neck.

Let these black bodies be free!

Passion and heart radiating out of my chest! My feet creating the heartbeat
of this here street.

Tap taping slide, step, bounce,

These feet hold me up when tired,

Cross me across finish lines

Not pictured for me.

Now they carry me across this concrete floor

Allowing me to leave my soul poured, mixed in with the sweat creating
evolutionary reflection puddles,

Staring back at me

Here is where I come to life

Here I feel in control and free.

The magic this body brews still leaves me in awe.

Breathless.

TREATING ME LIKE A WOMAN

I was three years old

My sister younger.

I was chosen

I was older.

He was a family friend

He lived next door.

He was a giant over me

Lifting, fondling, and that

Brush, I just can't recall how he used it.

I do remember that smell, it never leaves me.

Mama approaches,

He lifts me again, pulling me close,

Opening the oven door, he whispers in my ear

"I'll bake you, if you tell".

This became a locked file.

MAKE IT PLAIN

A new day

A clean page,

To write my story,

To make it plain.

Today I'll stand up to Yesterday.

I will not omit it,

For it happened.

I have decided to unloose myself,

From the chains that bind me.

To take back my authority

To declare that my pain from inflicted

Trauma did not stop me,

It Cannot stop me from choosing to live,

over waiting to die.

Fear no longer grips my heart sending me into one panic attack after another, spinning me into corners. That Shouts time out.

Regardless I continue to advance.

In the face of my mental illness,

I continue to come forth.

In freedom, my liberty.

UNFORGIVENESS!

Heavy baggage

Breaking me down!

Filled to the brim, spilling

Anger, resentment, and self- pity

charges me with faux control.

Foolery stalemates me.

Unforgiveness has deceived me,

sabotaged me. Blinding!

My motions hold back, instead of pushing forward.

Riddled by hits!

Still I long to live, I must let go,

The heavy baggage, ain't mine no way.

Processing. Why do I fight with the past?

No win there. Moments fleeing! Much time has passed.

I have decided, chose my future.

Freeing myself from past hurts, pain, and abuse.

Releasing all that has weighed me down.

I'm Lighter now, feels like freedom.

I have forgiven me, forgiven them.

I'll keep it moving!

like an eagle

My spirit soars now. I am Thirsty for Higher heights!

BABE GIRL YOU MINE

I labored for hours plus some.

My pain—enormous

I screamed, I gripped sheets,

I bared down and I moaned.

Every bit of pain was worth it.

More than diamonds

More than pearls

I labored to bring my girl in the world.

You are my blessing.

your miraculous life born out of GOD's love,

that chiseled your tiny little body and painted you

Chocolate. Your making was well conceived.

Created in GOD's image - you were worth it.

I watched you crawl until you walked.

I heard you say Mommy "I can do it,"

We called you Miss Can Do.

I heard you say, "Mommy, I genius"

I believed that you were.

When I told you that you were African, you raveled in it.

You would say "I African".

You will always be mine and forever live in my heart.

So don't you dare embrace the belief of another about you.

Don't you believe what they may say about you.

Your identity is in Christ!

Never, ever, give people that much power over your life.

They don't know you.

What they think they know

Barely touches the surface.

You my daughter have volumes,

They have yet to read a page.

REFLECTION

Spring has risen from under

The multilayered snow that's been anointing us day after day for weeks.

All I could see was white powder.

Riding down the 290, I see the brown naked trees sunbathing in all their
glory.

Teach me to be.

Just BE in my own, with a freedom and a peace of knowing it is what it's
going to BE, so Live

Bold now, but there are many seasons, and this one is

Not your last tale.

WAILING

Rachel "weeping for her children"

Her unsatiable wails

Like black mother's tears that bury

her children, lives ripped away,

Stolen because of the color of their skin.

Mothers left hollow inside,

Pain has taken residence.

Shattered Souls.

An endless scar that bleeds injustice.

TWILIGHT

Twilight, a time where night kisses day before it slips away.

I am raptured by its beauty,

stillness

A moment sur-real

I hear the echoes from my clock as each,

Second ticks away.

I can hear the cat's meow.

The wind whistles a tune.

I can see this maestro directing,

Tall weeds to move from one side

to the other, in unison

from my kitchen window.

An awesome wonder!

This is the perfect time for me!

I empty myself. Ready for the moment,

I talk and chat with the GOD of my soul.

The center of my world.

He fills me.

He becomes my strength and my salvation.

He is faithful!

He, who called me from the foundation of the world.

ITTY BITTY HUMAN

Grains. A grain lost in a dessert of options. You are seen, actually you have been perfected. You are looking at this picture the wrong way, you must step back, maybe tilt the frame, maybe close your eyes, take a deep breath and then reopen them wide. Do you see?

Do you see what I see? When we look into the sky, we see stars? The dimples placed into the night sky. And we are so far away that if you stretch your arm out and try to grasp one of those stars, we are naive to believe we can pinch one of those stars with our itty bitty fingers. Looking up, some would even say that stars look the size of a grain. You darling are a star, filled with ideas and passion, do not minimize yourself looking in the wrong mirror my friend.

THE TALL BLACK "SORTA CHOCOLATE MAN WITH GOLDEN UNDERTONES"

The tall black

Sorta chocolate man with

Golden undertones.

Yes! That's the one

He held my hand,

As I jumped each chain

That fenced the yard in

This day I fell,

I tried jumping over one of the

Chains, fell, splitting my chin open

Blood poured

The tall black

Sorta chocolate man, with golden undertones

Rushed to me, gently picking me up

Drew me near,

He held my tiny hand, I made no sound

As the doctor stitched me up

Touching the scar today, reminds me of my fall and

the tall black, sorta chocolate man with golden undertones

My first buck billington parade

He cheered me on as

I danced to the Madison Time

He was always there

Through the sunshine and the rain

Holding my tiny hand

The tall black, sorta chocolate man with golden undertones

Ravaged by Parkinson's is now asking

Me to hold his hand

I rushed to him, grasping his hand

Gently. Not ever wanting to let it go.

That Tall Black, sorta chocolate man with golden undertones

Is a great man.

You see he is my daddy.

MY RIDE OR DIE

I rose this morning to fine Meco,

My ride or die, sitting on the corner of our bed.

An unusual position

This was an unusual day.

One day after George Floyd was murdered

I went to him,

Babe what's wrong?

Tears fell like rain

Broken, Endangered Toy Soldier

Cried a river today.

I tried soothing him,

I told him I love you

I told him that "I love the

Golden skin that you are in".

His bottled-up feelings of

Rage, anger, and pain toward

A country with no love for the

Black man was seeping out.

THIS ROOM

this room

was filled by Black men

POWER

hailed from this room

BLACK MEN were tender with each other

Talented men,

all worthy of their calling

their gestures, their eyes, their smiles, their WORDS

Spoke character,

On one accord, they spoke of a shared history

That drew them close

Today in this room,

they joined, they discovered the determination and perseverance

their ancestors possessed, a substance their descendants inherited

a rhythm that moves them forward

Courageous In view of trepidation,

they continue

To rise and fall

One body, one spirit, one love

Fierce, yet gentle Black Men

In this room.

BIRTHDAY PARTY

My daughter surprised me,

She gave me a surprised birthday party.

once home, I walked into

greeters and into everyone singing happy birthday.

My daughter invited her entire third grade class

They were my guest.

Best party ever!

BLACK

Will my love be enough?

For my daughter's journey

In a world that have defined black

As valueless.

will my embrace,

dripping with sweet dark chocolate

be enough to cover her from

those resenting the rich hue of her skin.

Will my love fill her up, with substance,

that will stand in this world?

Will it be enough to endure hurtful words hurled like stones?

They pretend that we are invisible

It Hurts!

Will my love be enough?

KINDER GARDEN

Ms. Lopez sent a note home with babe gurl,
She said that my daughter took Tommy under her arms today
Helped him get through the day.
Ms. Lopez thought my daughter's actions were amazing,
She did not know that Babe gurl helps with her grandmother
who's going through the last stages of Alzheimer's,
Home care is costly, our family became the care blanket
That covers Mama, a labor of love
Babe gurl knows all 'bout caring.

BEST FRIEND

Brandi, invited to church by her best friend Samantha.

They sat together at church chit chatting

pastor Ron gave an altar call

Immediately they stopped the chatter.

They stood up, shared hands, and walked down

The center aisle to the alter.

Bowed heads and bowed knees as they offered their prayers at the alter

Brandi returned from the altar, this time sitting next to me

She whispered in my ear "Mommy, I left my snot and tears on the alter."

WHO IT BE?!

There goes the phone

I only let it ring once, because why not.

Who it Be?!

It be my mama!

My Black Queen!

My Ultimate Supreme!

It's my mama's voice.

The appreciation that came from no longer having the choice to see.

33 years out the womb and I popped out, her Rock Solid.

The world continuously tried my mama.

Me, little, watching that.

This little body, big mouth, and wise mind,

I was not having that.

"You too loud"

"You too dark"

"You too wild"

'Let me twist up your mind, have you feeling like a child

Your hips, your walk, how you demand with your talk.

All that needs to stop'

Mama, you had your own rhythm, a deep beat, with a unique Symphony.

It was your music I wanted to protect.

As your mini me – they do something to you,

They doing it to me times three.

When they tried to tone you down, It wouldn't matter if we was home,

or if we was in the streets,

I'd shout! "Live mama! You deserve to be Free!" Little me, just wanting you
to see you through my eyes not theirs.

I'm so proud of you mama, but I'm still over here shouting.

Live mama! Live Loud! Live Vibrant! And Live Free!

COULDN'T SEE MAMA

It wasn't until they told me

I couldn't see my mama,

when this pandemic became real for me

We didn't always see eye to eye,

but wasn't really supposed to.

The love was always there.

For a longtime it was me and mommy

Against the world.

I've gotten older and mommy got married.

So our lives grew like they were supposed to,

but this here connection will always

be ready to ride for one another

If tides ever come this way.

You don't realize how busy you live life

Until you're stripped,

In order to live.

The heavy thought of knowing

I could catch and carry something

that could bring death,

To my Joy,

Weighed on my heart

So I didn't.

I didn't see my mama.

2020 became many things for many people, but I rebuked

It being the year of loneliness for her.

Our voices connected every single day since

The first lockdown.

I did it, to keep my mama alive,

but it was me it saved.

TIME FOR A REFILL

Turned my heart upside down

And not even a penny fell

This must have been a rough week.

Charging everything to my heart,

Left me a little bankrupt,

But just for this week.

See the thing about it is,

My heart will never dry out,

Resiliency and passion refills

My soul like a youth fountain,

It continues to flow.

The aches of the world

I try to carry on my back,

But then my knees get weak.

The pains I can't heal, I try hard to absorb.

Let me take it, if only for the moment.

Soak it, in this empathetic sponge.

But right now, I'm all out.

I must curl up, cry out, and write.

Recharge. Buildup. And fill my heart again.

BREATH

He walked out and away
I stayed to watch myself
Sweat beaded, curled, and popped
On my forehead
Grunting and bearing down
My weight pressed down
Hard against the bed
That I lay on
Hands reaching and grasping
For something – anything
Catching and holding
The sheets – they became
My safety net
My screams became louder
I lost the sound of voices
Around me
When I returned
I heard voices
An octave above a whisper
Saying:
Breathe, now exhale
Each breath deeper and sharper
As my legs grew father apart
Life struggled to come forth
I could hear the words
I could feel the shouts
Crowing! I see the head
Push! Push! Push!
Pop!
Baby crying

OFFICER FRIENDLY!

Officer Parker met us

The same time each day

At the entrance of our school's door.

Knowing him made us feel secure

He was our Officer Friendly!

Many of us ran to him, waving our hands and shouting

"Hey Officer Parker, Hey Officer Parker"

Actually, what we were saying and meant is that,

We know you, Officer Parker

You matter to us!

We respected him,

I don't know if it was his

Navy blue uniform or

The relationship he shared with our parents.

Mamma & Daddy would be quite disappointed

if we showed officer Parker anything other than respect.

He earned our trust,

He cared not only about us

In the present,

He invested in our future.

He looked like us

We could be Officer Friendly

Protecting our community

We were encouraged and felt viable

We were visible,

He saw us!

THE CHILDREN

I see the children

Hands reaching up

Fingers stretched out

Trying to grasp

From a society greedy

In things

Poor in spirit

Please, look with me

See the children

THE CHOICE

I cannot see the children

Too many things

Plaguing their growth

Machines knocking

Down buildings

Like boulders

I cannot see the children

Too much dust in the way

A child peeks around the corner

Watching

Seeing

Bricks crash to the ground

Will she be buried?

Or have the chance to build

Now look

Each of us

To our fellowman

It is time to choose

Together – hand and hand

We can reach the children

LEFT OVER LOVE – ODE TO ALICE WALKER

You

I miss

I look at the black night

All that can be seen are

Bright lights

In tall skyscrapers

Again I sense the stillness,

My after hour

Company keeper

Wherever I turn:

You – are there

I can't touch you

Or even see you

I can only sense

The bare essence of you,

You whom I miss

BLACK CHILD

Who am I?
The black child closed up
Shut up and negated the
Opportunity
To learn to
Reach out
Speak out
Who am I?
The black child once released from
The wall that so tightly closed him in
Unable to secure a definite path for
The necessary knowledge was not there
To secure him
To learn to
Reach out
Speak out
Who am I?
The black child
Unaware of the socializing concept
Withdrawn, unable to touch the
Other person in
A communicative way
Who am I?

HANDS

I see the hands

It seems as thou they are

Reaching for me

From the sky

In my mind I really can see it

These hands

They are hands that

I know

Caring hands

Pushing for excellence hands

They touch my mind they touch my soul

They challenge me

To make a difference

In my life

Hands that challenge me

To just be me when

Touching someone else's

Soul

I do see them

In the sky

I want to reach back

For them

I want to meet these hands

If it's only my finger

Tips touching theirs

I want to reach the sky

Touch the hands

That reaches to pull

Me up

Pulling my spirit to higher ground

I say to higher ground

I envision this in my own mind

Surely this can be

Owned

Claimed

By me

RUNNING!

I tried counting each snow flake

The snow kept falling

I was unable

To count

Them all

I walked through the piles of snow

Leaving footprints

That melted quickly as though

I had never been there

The air is coarse

It refreshes me

I am thinking

Of things I didn't do

My rhythm quickens

My walk out chasing

My thoughts

My feet and tears

Are running now

Didn't go to prom

Didn't have rosy underwear

Didn't have many pictures showing me

Didn't wear perfume

Didn't really run the race

Held myself back from winning

Did have my writings

Still do

Today I want to be intimate with pretty

Has too much time escaped?

My fears grow

My tears flow

My steps hasten

The weather is rough

Matching the turmoil

Inside me

The snow cold on my face

Meets the hot feelings inside

Out here I need not hide

The tenderness in my eyes

Once I leave here to go inside

I'll need an excuse

INNER CITY SONG

I rose this morning

To mice running across my floor

Looking for crumbs and

To the noise

That seeped

Through my window

The noise

From garbage cans

As hands searched

For crumbs from

Yesterday's meal

The slamming noise

Of garbage can tops

Like loud cymbals

With drumming

Sending messages

The search

The chase

The noise

The melody

Nears completion

Yesterday's meal

Has become today's

Edge against hunger

The melody still

Rings in my ear

PSYCHEDELIC BLUE

As he silently appeared on

The banks of my memory

He bucked the unsettled turbulence

That had laid dormant

Releasing the fury of

Piled up irreconcilable

Yesterdays

I could hear his presence

As he drew nearer

I could feel him

As he became clearer

He was wearing psychedelic blue

Which reminded me that

Blue Monday was just one of seven

His baggage carried the pain

That tormented me and

Rose above my rationality

My understanding returned

Empty when looking for

Reason

My mind screamed!

My Husband

My Betrayer

FLOWERS

Budding flowers

Each bearing beauty

In her own truth

A brilliance shining

As we go forth

To mend the four corners

Of humanity

Awareness unveils compassion

Fires the furnace of our souls

Heating our spirits until

They rise and spill into

The threads that bond

The reason to search

We have traveled deep within

Gaining in truths

They are many

The grains of our memories

Are plenty

Like sand on windblown dunes

That builds the shores of today

Yesterday's fields are the threading

Grounds we have crawled, walked,

Run, and yes fallen upon

Still coming forward

Still coming on

We are different in our faces

We are one in spirit

We shed

We flourish

We are flowers

We dare to dream

Better tomorrows

Trembling with readiness

We come

Prepared to blossom

Prepared to carry forth

The warmth and light

Of knowledge give us,

Prepared to hope, to heal,

To bring to life

The dream

WARMTH

The hall where you walked

Is empty, we miss seeing you.

Elegance

You had plenty

Your laughter seemed

To lighten hearts

Seeking to ease into

The comfort of the day

Your strength was always present

As we stand here

Near to our minds

Are all the times

You invited us in

For quiet talks

Unfolding your substance

Sharing knowledge of past and present

We listened closely

As you inspired us

Gently touched us

With the depth of your

Words and the warmth

Of your heart

We joined you

For a moment

On your journey

Parting ways

We wish you well

THRESHOLD

Today the doors of two separate

Lives have closed to open one

Our love for each other has

Brought us to this threshold

Where we stand awaiting thee

We envision ourselves

Walking together in your

Field unharmed

Abiding in your love as our cover

As we awaken into the deeps of

How great thou are

In drawing nearer to each other

We draw nearer to thee

Underneath our flesh

We tremble from the

Might of your words,

Yet we are eager to

Receive our vows

Standing at the passageway

We embrace each other

Two lives joining and becoming one

Standing in your glory

The strength of your love will

Order the steps that we climb

As we enter the doors of tomorrow

PERCEPTION

He laid there silent

Eyes closed –

No more:

Reception

Pre - perception

Perception of the reality of this life

Dressed in his best apparel

One would think

As though he picked it himself

Face grim

First time he didn't wear a smile

He wore bold colors, when I saw him

I am sure he would have chosen

Brighter ones today

Dull and unflavored talk did not

Speak the joy he illuminated

Well, what do you expect,

When others attempt to tell

Your story, shows they barely

Touch the surface

DISTORTION

Feathers plucked from
My very wing.
Images of society trying to
Dismantle me

HEY BLACKIE

Hey Blackie!

Who you talking to?

I am dark and lovely.

My hue is pure, deep and rich.

Haven't you heard?

The darker the berry

The sweeter the juice.

SUGA' BABE

When you were so very tiny and tender,

I drew you close,

My beautiful Suga' Babe

I saw you and still do

You're courageous, with fire in your veins,

You came here believing in great possibilities

GOD gave me a miracle, you

You would say to me,

no matter the size of the task,

I can do it, Mamma! I can do it!

Remember, Shout, Let the world know

you're here!

ROLES

This Mental illness has taken residence in me

It's cutting me deep

in the midst of raising babe gurl

my emotional intelligence

declined,

burned, like overcooked chicken gizzards

my daughter was so young

What did she know,

She knew exactly what to do

Must have been here before,

Our roles, exchanged.

My head in her itsy bitsy lap

As she read one of her primary school books

She read to me,

"I will love you forever.

I will love you for always".

She kept on going,

One word after another

I will love you forever.

I will love you for always.

Thinking now,

I stole from her

What I should have been giving her.

Please forgive me.

S o r r y...

PUSH & PULL

When someone says that they will take them some

Is it different from someone saying they will give you some?

Bottom or top, does it matter?

That push and pull can really interfere with

Your perception of women and their liberties

METAPHOR

This place was built off of bad thoughts and
tainted ideas.
If we are teaching that mere
mortals can create a new beginning just by
waking up and taking a new breath, why do we
keep Earth?
In the beginning when ground was
green, trees were strong, and sky was blue with
remixes of peach and mango colors depending
on the decision of the fire star that rises and sets
around us. Why do we keep earth?
Who named It that?
The same men that are incomplete and stubborn.
Men who believe they are Earth, and
everything else revolves around them like the
Sun. Feeding and nourishing them
Leaving everyone around them biting at their crumbs?

OIL MY SCALP

Hair Grease

Here we sit

Sit on this carpeted floor

My head laying down on mama's crossed legs

We both watching the show.

you already know, something funny, something Black.

Palms seasoned with love, my mama rubs my back.

After years of, 'We gon' make it.'

Here we are, in the moment, present.

Present and free with one another, allowed to breathe.

Mama now rubbing my hair, looks down at me, then kisses me on my forehead.

Still sitting on that floor, our mother and child energies intertwining around us like

a luminating force protecting us, from the outside adversity of an insecure world.

Who for whatever reason hates the Black woman, but not now, not in that room,

not on that floor.

This moment was for us, for us to love and breathe.

Still sitting on that floor, mama picks up that comb.

My eyes on the tv.

Mama begins to oil my scalp.

Now that is a Black love language all on its own.

Peace, Love, and Hair grease.

GET UP OFF ME

Misunderstood Misguided

Blindsided, Oh Wait,

Allys?

They hate me

Think this dark skin, something

Like fresh Hot Chocolate…

(Smells) enticing, Looks good

But they try to swallow the idea

Of me too quick!

Get up off me!

They burn themselves

They've got me all wrong.

But because of the fetish of

Being an ally without said work,

Hurt.

Burned their little throat

Now I'm comforting them.

How?

Come here, lie thy head on my bosom

It'll be alright, I swear I'm not hot

I'm actually good once you get to

Know me.

Listen to me plead

Sound like I'm down on my knees

Please ally don't oust me.

Disgusting,

Get up off me.

2021

This seed's been laying beneath the dirt for a long time. Doing what seeds know

How to do, making the best out of a seedy situation. Who knows if it'll ever sprout.

For some seeds the peak is the dirt, and even then there are levels.

But 2021, I feel it, it's not even the peak

But my entire life is about to change. Hey Change, pick me up on your way back up.

Lord I'm going to bust out of this shell, and reach as high as I can.

Maybe I can make it, maybe past the ground line, make it to air.

Please Protect me.

Guide me.

Allow me to remain ambitious and trust my gut.

Make me pretty.

Let me feel like a prince in a dress.

Take me with you.

Allow my ideas and drive to sail me threw the Oceans, with enough room for

Mom, Mike, and pup.

Take me. I'm ready for this journey.

DEAR MAMAS

I want to start this with how much I love you #Period.

Man, to be a mom is pouring everything that is inside of you,

letting it pour from the depths of you

out through your fingertips.

Pouring it into pitchers. And after you've

given all that you have, twisted your arms tight enough to get all the last drips out

through your fingertips, into those pitchers, you stand, not looking at what's beside

you and what's behind you, you just see what's in front of you and it's those pitchers, you

take those pitchers that you just filled, and with both hands, because of course, you were draining through both hands, and pouring all of you through all 10 fingertips. And there's

still strength in you to stand over these pitchers, now you pick up these overflowing

pitchers and begin pouring these two bottomless pitchers, where are you pouring them,

why did you give your all and drain all of you, then I see, the seeds that you have created?

they needed a little watering, and momma decided I'm going to pour everything that is in

me onto you, sometimes the sun might not shine in your direction, and I'm going to shift

you, you'll think I'm getting in your way, but my seed needs light, sometimes I might sing

to you in the early morning before the sun has awakened, you'll be stressed, wondering

why, but I know there'll be times you'll feel alone, and need a voice to guide you back to

be reminded of how much you're worthy, and of how special you are, and in case you forget how much you need you (because that happens), I'll say follow your mothers

voice back to reset, ground, get your balance, and then fly away again. You are bigger

then any situation #period. Happiness is a compelling chase drawn by someone still

chasing it. We must be honest, transparent, realistic, imaginative, and direct in the

moment. This is a new time and we're no longer chasing white picket fences. Now we are learning to love ourselves and understand ourselves, which is a lifetime journey,

nothing figured out at the blink of an eye, but please give yourself time. I love you

SINK

Every time I look

There's a Duck missing.

I might just stop looking,

Fighting hard to keep it together

But Baby, this levee

Is about to break,

Flooding these mental

And emotional gates

Save me,

Life jacket me please

This fool can't float.

Ducks in a row,

Mine keeps missing.

All this weight

My shoulders lifting,

Chil' please.

These thighs and hips

Could carry ships

But yet I'm still drowning

Help me.

I got this, I been getting

This, since

Got had sense

I got it.

Breathe, we got it

Float

WORK

My tears are silent

Dried up

Behind smiles, leaving tense temples and salt lines

Energy wasted pretending

True Feelings neglected

For what? For whom?

Take more work

BIG WAL-MART

We Tricked Massa'

Got the Cow by its tongue

And it's money.

Straight money

Hungry streets

But we slipped in

Like mice and decided

Mouth wide, clenched down

We gon' eat

Big wall street.

We knocking,

Government failed,

Pandemic 10 months

Famished forever.

Came over as slaves

Refused us education,

Snatched our names, and bloodlines

Chained and beat. The names

In a book next to the liquor

Big wall street always been the same.

But bitch

We snuck on the block

Knock knock,

It's hungry Americans at your door

We got your ass.

Fuck you, now pay me.

We out here still hungry.

FEELS CLICHÉ

Needing a vibe, trying to catch a wave.

That's just cliche things people say,

But we know that need, that feeling

Been wanting to drag my hand

With this pen to this paper all day,

But the more I guilt about it

The thicker the air between my hand

With this pen and this paper gets.

Checking off fake list, and doing

Everything everyone else needs,

Because I need this. Now here

I finally am. 10:25pm, 3 days later.

Finally letting this pen dance, and ink run.

No destination really planned, just hope

It doesn't take so much work to visit these

Pages again.

STRIP

I want to be so vulnerable that our bones are chaffing from

Being so wrapped around one another from no longer needing clothes,
skin, or walls.

SELF-TALK

"You a friendly bitch, but you are still black, bitch, and you a dom bitch, don't

you be a too friendly black dom bitch, Message heard..."

A PHONE CALL

Thank you for your call. I was pretty hesitant to answer as I was entangled with

self-harming thoughts that stretched across my mind like tight thread,

Spider web,

Made of thin cut glass.

Right when you were calling, I was painfully forcing pieces of my body through

this glass like webs.

Arm straight. Bleeding from the skin being scrapped off like cheese or soft butter

sliced off for afternoon lunch.

I'm hurting. I was hurting then you called. Thank you, mom. I really wanted to

hurt, but I didn't. Like I was already hurting

But I wanted to change the direction of the pain, something I could control.

Something I could stop. Something that I could …

I thought about killing myself

And then you called.

I'm still hurting. But the pain is not throbbing as hard. The sadness isn't as

loud.

But to a controllable sadness

I am glad I didn't kill myself at that moment. I'm still hurting. But it's not as

loud. I can cover up this noise with louder noise that I create to distract, made

up of the joyous sounds.

REAL TIME

Reality has shown me that with all my movement,

I've gotten nowhere.

Two steps forward

One step backward

This became the rhythm of my life

Self-sabotage, the name of the dance

Getting nowhere

It was not until my desires demanded change.

Did my life began to sway to a new

Rhythm?

Loosing myself from a past

that looked down on me,

instead of lifting me up.

I faced my mental illness from a different view this time,

I embraced it, decided to take this journey.

Not knowing if I would be a midget or a giant.

Not caring about the stigma anymore.

I will journey with the unknowing to discover more of me.

Excited that I am learning a new dance.

Excited that I continue.

Regardless of fear

I have hope,

That quiets my spirit.

WHY FEAR DIFFERENCE

Why is it that fear overtakes you?

Threatens you!

When you lack understanding to difference?

The unknown becomes your Goliath,

Slaying you.

CONDITIONING

I heard your talk shooting through electromagnetic waves of frequency,

Bullets whistling and slicing air, I saw your images transmitted, influencing, and conditioning. A chastened potential, splashed by hatred.

Killing more souls than war claimed bodies.

You've colored me and my representation ugly

As if my creation was begotten from your

Ill talk & empty images.

My identity, my image, who I am

Was created before the foundation of the earth

Before you were thought of

You have no say. I am divinely created.

MENTAL

Piled up jet black yesterdays
Cascaded on me,
a horrendous waterfall.
Inflicting my mental health,
Leaving me, the keeper of this house
Emotionally lifeless, unable to quiet me.
Scared to call out, help!
Insecurity pushed out esteem.
Trampled by fear, it chased me.
I couldn't run fast enough from myself.
My behavior erratic, panic attacks,
Whenever I tried standing, so I crawled.
With the right help, now I am walking,
With purpose.
empowered to
discover who I am and to
discover the power that I possess.
My character reflects the quality of much
Invested work that I continue to do, in my discovery of me.

ABOUT THE AUTHORS

Brandi Kneedly

I am my mother's child, battered and nourished through my own life experiences, seasoned with my truth. My mother and I talked for years about doing a project together. Sometimes the idea is so grand, that you do not even want to touch it. We motivated and encouraged one another to see our individual projects through, and I am so glad we allowed our pens to meet and write our truths out on shared pages. Our relationship was never perfect, but our love was never missing. I am blessed to have built the kind of relationship that we have now. I am a creative soul, and I don't ever see myself stopping; and I have my mother to thank for that. Stay blessed.

Breinda Crosby-Averhart

My life is anchored by a foundation greater than I.

It is the Joy of the LORD that strengthens me to rise up out of my traumatic circumstances.

I would have succumbed to life struggles without it.

I pray my daughter love, for love never fails, and I pray she inherits my strengths and none of my idiosyncrasies.

Made in United States
Orlando, FL
27 December 2021

12594890R00068